Copyright ©2024 Conchetta Park

Written by Conchetta Park
Illustrated by Shany Ahmed

Photograph of Conchetta Park by Joy Masi
Photograph of Shany Ahmed by Lilit

Published by Miriam Laundry Publishing Company
miriamlaundry.com

All rights reserved. This book or any portion thereof may not be reproduced or used in any manner whatsoever without the express written permission from the author except for the use of brief quotations in a book review.

HC ISBN 978-1-77944-144-7
PB ISBN 978-1-77944-143-0
e-Book ISBN 978-1-77944-142-3

FIRST EDITION

To my Cosmic Family, who I chose to do this journey with—may we all remember who we truly are.

Before Celeste was born, she lived far, far away among the stars. There, Celeste could climb and fly and swing from star to star

and dance along the Universe.

She loved the tickling feeling in her tummy every time she connected with the wind in her hair, the rhythm in her body, and the energy of the stars.

She wasn't afraid of anything!

But when Celeste became a little girl, she was afraid of many things. Sometimes, she wouldn't play games with her friends at the park because she was afraid.

She was afraid to go down the big slide.
She was afraid to go on the teeter-totter.
She was afraid to use the swings for big kids.

What if I am not able to do what the other kids are doing? What if I fall? The heights scare me! Celeste thought.

One day, as she left school, Celeste's friend Carmelita caught up to her. "Would you like to come to my birthday party?"

Celeste's eyes grew big with excitement.

"Sure!" She loved birthday cake and ice cream and all kinds of party games. Celeste couldn't wait to have fun with her friends.

Except …

The party wasn't at Carmelita's house.

The party was at a rock-climbing playground!

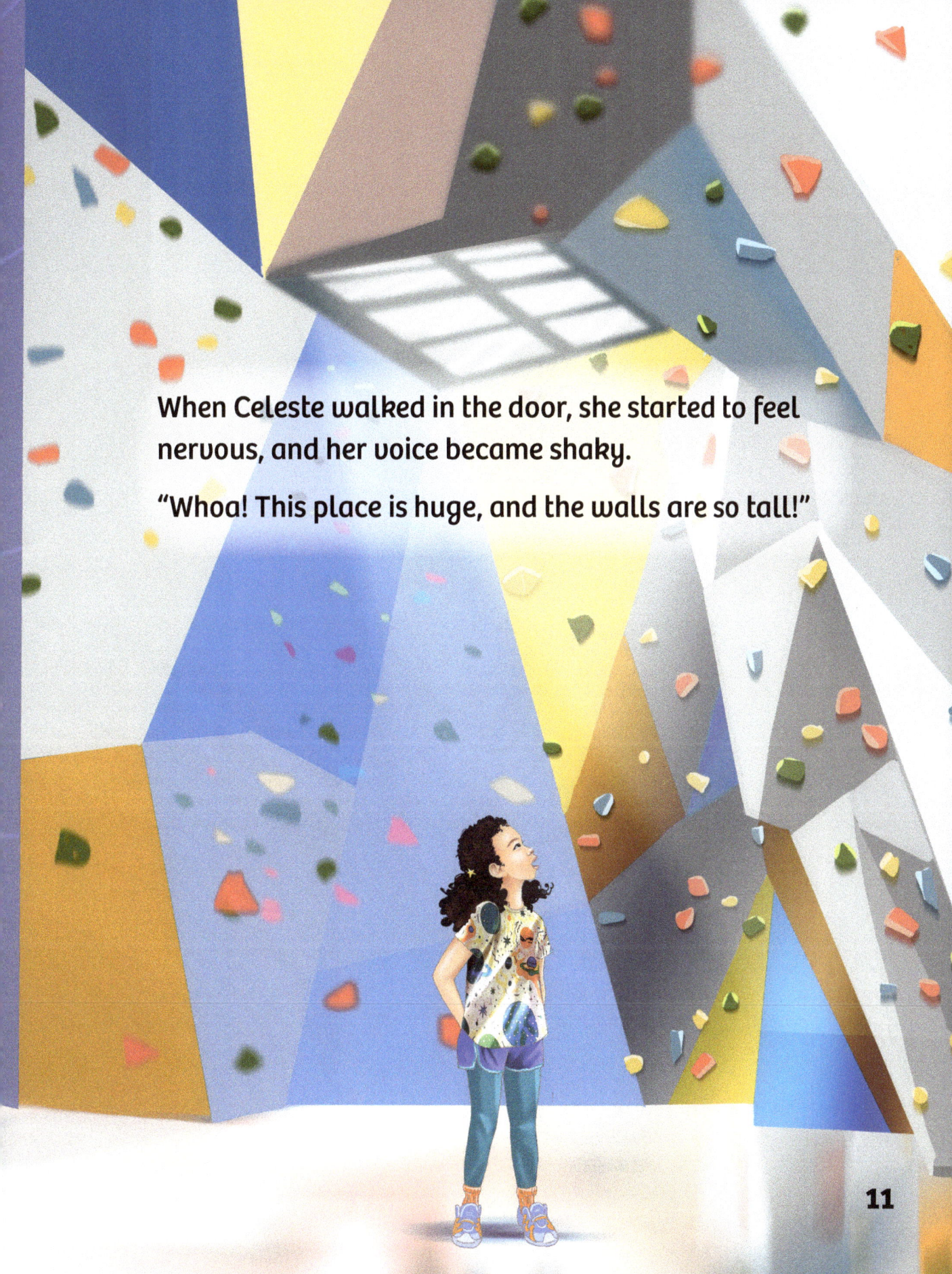

When Celeste walked in the door, she started to feel nervous, and her voice became shaky.

"Whoa! This place is huge, and the walls are so tall!"

Celeste watched Carmelita climb the rocks on the wall. She got all the way to the top and then swung back down to the floor. The other birthday guests were all doing the same thing.

"Celeste!" Carmelita called. "Are you ready to climb the wall? You're up next!"

Celeste looked up at the wall. It seemed very safe. No one was falling or getting hurt. *They're all having fun, so maybe I can do it too*, she thought.

"Yes!" Celeste finally answered. "I'm ready for my turn."

As she put on the harness and safety pads, Celeste felt her heart beating faster and faster. Her palms became sweaty.

What if I slip? Her body froze.

But Celeste heard her friends cheering her on, and she didn't want to disappoint them.

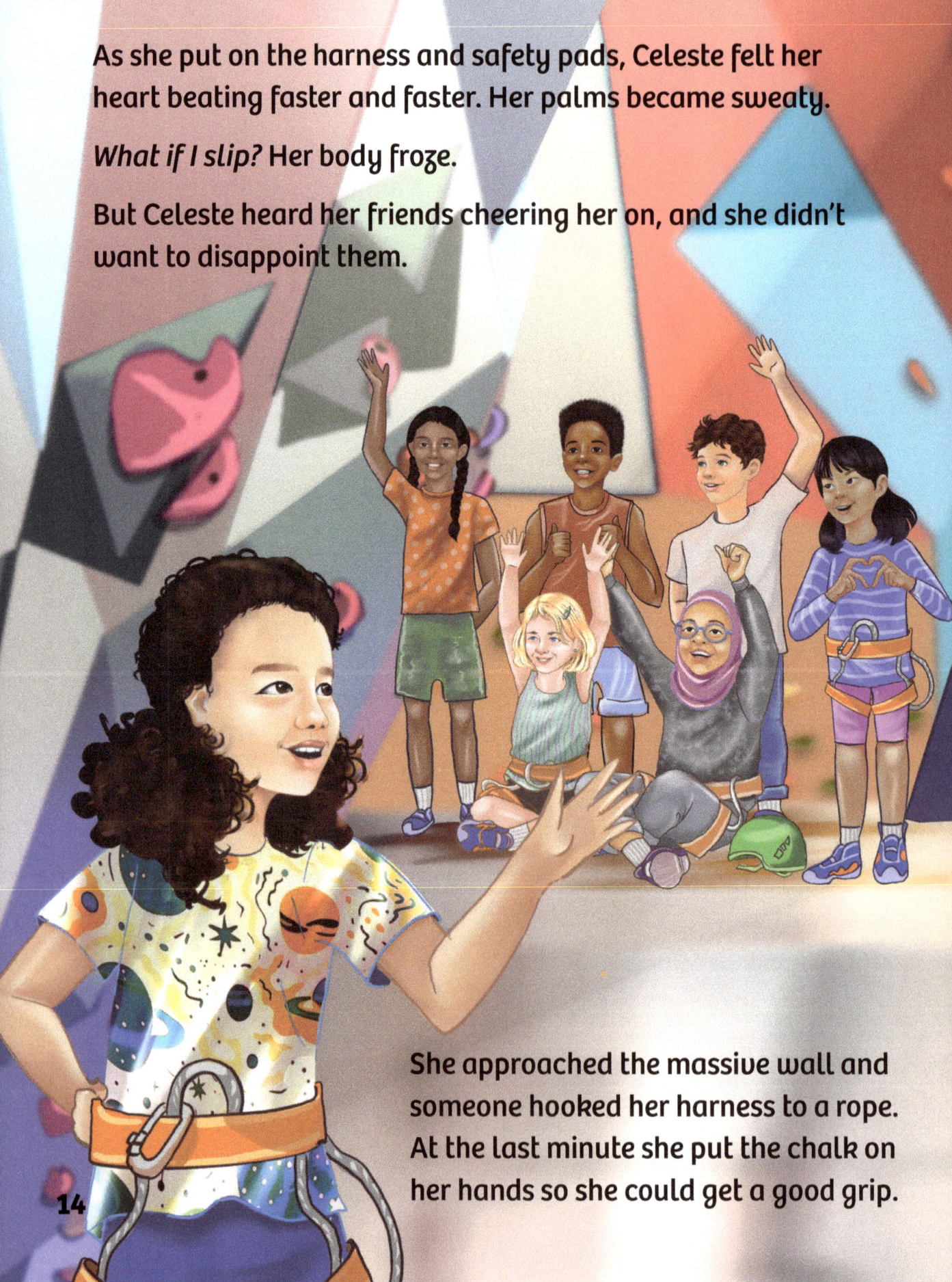

She approached the massive wall and someone hooked her harness to a rope. At the last minute she put the chalk on her hands so she could get a good grip.

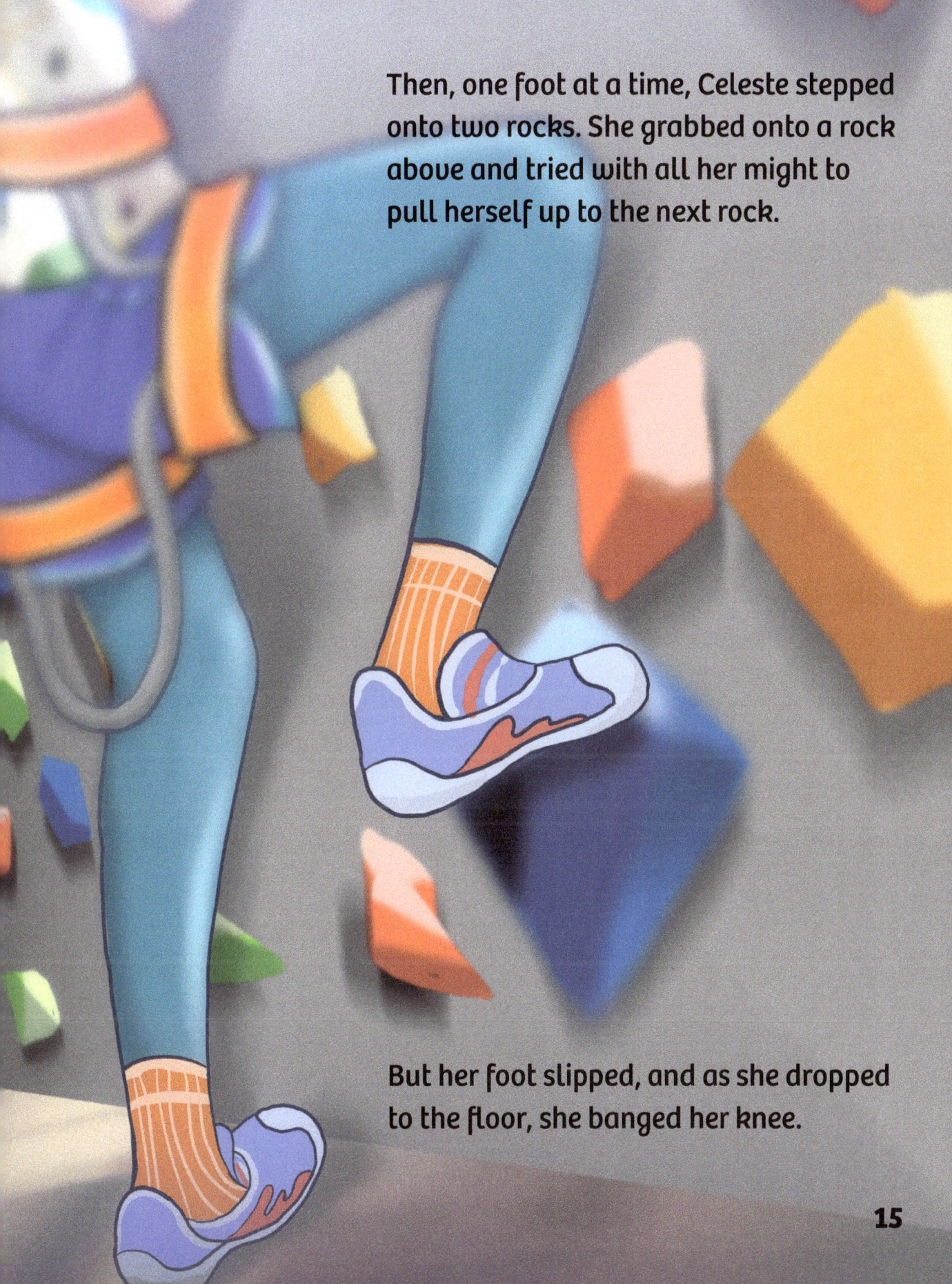

Then, one foot at a time, Celeste stepped onto two rocks. She grabbed onto a rock above and tried with all her might to pull herself up to the next rock.

But her foot slipped, and as she dropped to the floor, she banged her knee.

"Ouch!" Celeste yelled, rubbing her burning knee.

Carmelita called to her. "Are you okay?"

"I ... I think so." Celeste got up, took a deep breath, and tried to climb the wall again. She gripped each rock with all her might and managed to move just the littlest bit up the wall.

But then ... Celeste looked down! *I'm up so high,* she thought. *It's like the big slide at the park!* She missed her step and dropped down again! This time, the pulley caught her, and Celeste swung gently.

"Isn't it fun?" Carmelita asked.

And much to her surprise, Celeste thought it *was* fun!

Celeste started climbing again. One hand, one foot. One hand, one foot. As she made her way up the wall, higher and higher, shaking with each step, Celeste did not look down. She kept her head looking up and as she did that, she felt a tickling feeling in her stomach.

She started to remember a time when she could fly—a time when she could jump from star to star without fear of falling.

A time when she had no doubt that she could not do it and, most importantly, when she had fun jumping and flying.

Celeste loved the tickling feeling it gave her in her stomach when she discovered something new.

Suddenly, Carmelita shouted, "Celeste, you did it!"

Celeste snapped out of her memory and glanced around.

"I did it! I made it to the top!"

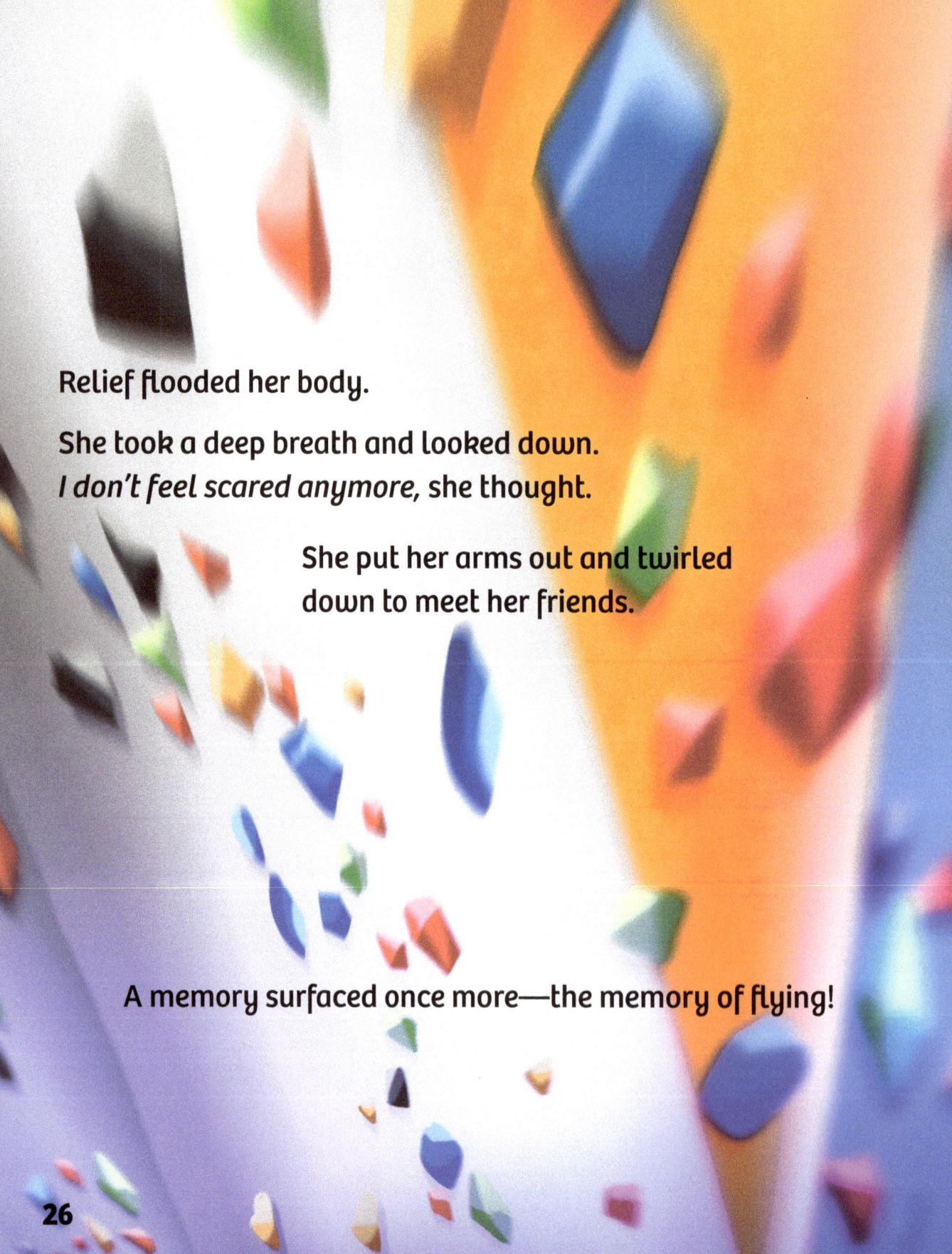

Relief flooded her body.

She took a deep breath and looked down.
I don't feel scared anymore, she thought.

She put her arms out and twirled down to meet her friends.

A memory surfaced once more—the memory of flying!

Before the party ended, Celeste climbed the rock wall two more times. And then, as she ate birthday cake and danced with her friends, Celeste felt that little tickle in her stomach.

She knew she was happy.

On her way home, Celeste bent down to pick up something shiny on the ground. It was a little silver star.

Celeste tilted her head to the night sky and smiled.

About the Author

C. Park is from Philadelphia where she currently resides. Her love for story time and picture book literature sparked from her experience as a substitute kindergarten teacher. Her aim is to remind people that they all have that inner whisper that knows they can do all things. When she is not working on writing children's books, C. Park loves to be near the ocean and to drink enough water!

To learn more visit:
lucis-corner.com

About the Illustrator

Shany is a self-taught multidisciplinary artist who is profoundly inspired by folklore and mythology. Her work frequently taps into the relationship between nature, cultures and femininity.

Shany lives in Kuala Lumpur, Malaysia.
To learn more about her work go to:
manje.pb.studio